It's not fair!

Kitty looked round the playground, at all the children running around. Some tall, some small. Some fat, some thin. Some dark, some fair. Some shy, some bold. Some who could sing, some who could swim. Some dainty, some clumsy . . .

'We're *all* different,' she said to herself, 'and I suppose *that's* fair!'

BEL MOONEY

It's not fair!

Illustrated by
Margaret Chamberlain

mammoth

First published in Great Britain 1989
by Methuen Children's Books Ltd
Published 1991 by Mammoth
an imprint of Egmont Children's Books Limited
Michelin House, 81 Fulham Road, London SW3 6RB

Reprinted 1991, 1992 (three times), 1993 (three times),
1994 (twice), 1995 (three times), 1996 (four times), 1997 (twice),
1998 (twice)

ISBN 0 7497 0575 2

A CIP catalogue record for this title
is available from the British Library

Printed and bound in Great Britain
by Cox & Wyman Ltd, Reading, Berkshire

Contents

It's not fair!

...that I'm little

Kitty was the smallest girl in her class. Usually she did not care. She could swim well, and run as fast as most people – well, almost – and once came first in the egg and spoon race on Sports Day. So it did not matter – being small. That was what Kitty thought.

But one day something happened to make her change her mind. It was one of those days when nothing went right.

First of all, there was a new boy in Kitty's class. His name was Tom, and he was very, very tall. Kitty didn't like him very much, because he called her 'Shrimp'.

The whole class was working on a mural in paint and cut-out paper, and on this day Kitty and Tom and two other children were chosen to do special extra work on it.

Kitty was very excited. She loved painting – especially when you could be really messy.

That was 'why she wanted to paint the sky, with lovely big fluffy clouds floating along. But each time she tried Tom laughed at her. 'You can't reach,' he said. 'You're too small.' And he leaned over her head, and did the bit she wanted to do.

At break she found someone had put her

jacket on one of the higher pegs she could not reach, and she wouldn't ask Tom or anyone to get it down. So she went outside without it, and felt cold. Then the playground helper told her off for not wearing a coat.

'I couldn't reach it,' said Kitty, in a small voice.

'Oh, you're such a *dear little* thing,' said the lady, nicely.

Kitty sighed. It really was not fair.

Then it was the games lesson, when the girls had to play netball. They were learning to stop each other getting the ball. You had to dodge quickly, and jump very high. Kitty wasn't very good at that.

Today she was worse than ever. She did not get hold of the ball once. All the other girls had longer arms and legs, and it seemed easy for them. Afterwards one of the girls said something that hurt Kitty very much. 'No one will want you in their team, Kitty. You're too *tiny*!'

Kitty was very quiet when she got home. Her mum noticed. At last Kitty burst into tears. 'It's not fair that I'm little,' she sobbed.

Kitty told her mum everything. Mum nodded. 'It isn't easy. *I* was small when I was a little girl, and you ask Daniel what

they say to him in school!'

Surprised, Kitty went to find her big brother to ask him. He made a face. 'They sometimes call me Shorty,' he said. 'But it's always very friendly, so I don't mind!'

'Are you small too?' asked Kitty.

'Yes. But I'd rather be me than the boy in our class who's so tall and thin they call him Stringy!'

'You see,' said Mum, 'most people have got something about themselves they would

10

like to change. When you know that, it makes you feel better about yourself.'

Kitty thought about that, and she made a plan. The next day, at playtime, she made herself feel brave enough to go up to Tom when he was standing on his own.

'Tom, can I ask you something?' she said.

'What, Shrimp?'

'If you had one wish, what would you change about yourself?'

The tall boy looked surprised. Then he went pink, and whispered, 'My hair. I *hate* my hair.' Kitty looked at it. It was orangey-brown. She thought it was rather nice.

'At my old school they called me Carrots,' he said, 'and it wasn't *fair*. But don't you tell anyone, will you – Shrimp?'

Kitty said she wouldn't.

Then she found Susie, the big strong girl who had said Kitty was no good at netball, and asked her the same question. Susie frowned, and answered quickly. 'My size,' she said, 'because I feel like an elephant. I'd like to be smaller. I'd like to be like *you*.'

'Like me?' squeaked Kitty, amazed.

Susie nodded.

Kitty looked round the playground, at all the children running around. Some tall, some small. Some fat, some thin. Some dark, some fair. Some shy, some bold. Some

who could sing, some who could swim. Some dainty, some clumsy . . .

'We're *all* different,' she said to herself, 'and I suppose *that's* fair!'

It's not fair!

... that people can't take a joke

'Kitty! You're the naughtiest child in England!' said Mum.

'How do you know? You haven't met them all,' said Kitty.

'Oh, very clever,' said Mum, in her irritated voice.

'Thanks, Mum!' said Kitty.

Her mother opened her mouth – then closed it again. Kitty thought she looked like a fish, and said so. It made her laugh. Then

Mum got up from the table, and started to come towards her – so Kitty thought it was time to leave the room.

She ran into the hall, and up the stairs, bumping into Dad, who was walking down. He dropped his book with a crash, and it tumbled to the bottom of the stairs, bending its cover back.

'Oh, be careful, Kitty,' he shouted. 'Look where you're going!'

'*You* could see me coming,' retorted Kitty.

'That's not the point,' said Dad.

'Yes it is,' said Kitty, ''cos if *you* don't see, why should *I* look?'

Dad frowned. 'I'm not standing here arguing with you, Kitty,' he said, 'because I think you're a very cheeky little girl.'

And with that he stomped off down the stairs and closed the sitting-room door with a slam.

This time Kitty didn't laugh.

On the landing she met Daniel, her brother, coming out of his room wearing his new glasses. He didn't like his glasses, at all, even though he only really had to wear them for reading.

Kitty giggled.

'Hallo, *Wol*,' she said.

'What?' said Dan, puzzled.

'Wol,' she smiled. 'You know, in the Pooh Bear story – it's how poor old owl spelt his own name. WOL!' She giggled.

Daniel knew what she meant right away, and his face went red. 'I don't look like an owl,' he said, in his crossest voice. 'And even if I did you shouldn't say so. It's nasty.'

Then he rushed past her down the stairs, with angry clattering footsteps.

Kitty was still smiling, but the smile froze on her face. Slowly she walked into her own room, and looked into the mirror. She felt as if everybody in the house was against her.

The trouble with people (she thought) is that they never understand jokes. She wasn't trying to be nasty, or cheeky, or clever. She was only trying to be funny, and that was different.

'It's just not *fair*,' she said to her own frowning reflection. 'None of them can take a joke.'

Then she thought of the way Dad and Dan teased her, and expected her to smile with them . . . And it was then that Kitty had her Great Idea.

An hour later it was time for lunch. She heard Dad calling her name, and she went slowly downstairs, sitting at the table without a word.

Nobody in Kitty's house stayed cross for long, and so Dad smiled at her. 'What have you been doing upstairs, Kit?' he asked.

'Just reading,' she replied, in a polite, flat voice – not at all like her own, 'and tidying my room.'

'Gosh, are you feeling all right?' joked her mother, as she passed the plates.

'Oh yes, I'm fine, thank you,' said Kitty in the same voice.

Daniel looked at her strangely. He had taken his glasses off now, and seemed to have forgotten her joke. 'Do you want to play football after lunch?' he asked.

'No, thank you,' Kitty said quietly. 'I don't want to get dirty.'

All through the meal it was the same. Kitty was quiet and polite – and very, *very* dull. She never once smiled, or laughed, or giggled, or teased, or talked with her mouth full, or any of the things that made her *Kitty*. She said 'yes, please' and 'no, thank you' as if they were strangers and she had to be on her best behaviour.

By the time they had finished the meal, the other three were looking at her with astonishment.

'Are you sure you're not feeling poorly?' asked her mother, sounding really worried.

'You're not my normal little Kit,' said her dad.

'Kitty – you're being really *boring*,' grumbled Dan.

At that, Kitty got to her feet. 'Right!' she said, and folded her arms. 'Listen! When I'm being jokey and teasing you all, you don't like it. Then when I'm quiet and polite and serious you don't like that either. Do you think that's fair?'

'Er – no,' said Dad.

'Not really,' said Mum.

Daniel just shook his head.

Kitty was triumphant. 'There you are then,' she said. 'So you have to decide which sort of *me* you want to have around.

It's only fair.'

Dad smiled. 'Oh, I know what I think,' he said, and Mum smiled too, nodding before he had spoken. 'I'd rather have the Kitty who's the funniest girl in the world.'

'How do you know?' grinned Kitty.
''Cos you don't know all the rest!'

It's not fair!

. . . that he goes to bed late

It happened the same way every evening. Mum came into the sitting room and tapped Kitty on the shoulder. 'Time for bed, love,' she said.

Kitty scowled and pointed to where Dan was reading, or drawing or watching some television. 'Tell him, too,' she said.

Mum sighed. 'It's not Daniel's bed-time,' she said.

'That's not fair,' Kitty wailed. 'He always stays up later than me.'

'That's because he's older than you are,' said Mum. 'Honestly, Kitty, I shouldn't have to say that again.'

And then Kitty gave in, and went upstairs as slowly as possible, muttering dark things about her brother and how it wasn't fair that being older gave you treats – and so on.

But then came a night when the story was different. Two weeks earlier a new family

21

had moved in next door, and Kitty was pleased that amongst their three children was a boy who was exactly her age. He was called William. They liked the same games, and soon found out everything about each other.

So when Kitty's mother came to send her to bed Kitty looked up and said, 'It isn't fair.'

'I don't believe it!' said Mum. 'I've *told* you Dan is older and that's why . . .'

'Ah,' said Kitty. 'I'm not talking about him. I'm talking about William! He goes to bed only half an hour before Daniel does, and William is *exactly my age*.'

'Oh,' said Mum.

There was a short silence.

Kitty was triumphant. 'So I think I should be allowed to stay up as long as William.'

'All families have different rules, Kitty,' said Mum.

'I don't think that's fair,' said Kitty.

'Well, all children need different amounts of sleep,' said Mum, 'and that's got nothing to do with fairness!'

'Some people need to eat less food than others, too,' said Dad, from behind his newspaper.

All that week Kitty kept on. And on. Each night she complained. She asked Dad what he thought, and he agreed with Mum – of course. She asked Daniel – and he was on her side.

She even asked William's mother if she thought it was fair that she had to go to bed earlier than William. Mrs Jones looked embarrassed. 'That's up to your mummy, Kitty,' she said.

At last Kitty's mother could stand it no

longer. She had been busy and by Sunday
night she was tired. So when Kitty started to
say, 'Can't I stay up a little bit longer, as late
as . . .' Mum interrupted.

'ALL RIGHT! We'll do an experiment.
This week you can stay up till Dan's
bed-time, which is later than William's.
That way, he'll start telling *his* mum it's not
fair, which will make a change – and *you* can
see how much sleep you need.'

'Oh, Mum. THANKS,' Kitty gasped.

It was wonderful to stay up late that night – as if it was Christmas or New Year. Kitty felt very grown-up. And the next morning she didn't feel a bit tired. 'You see, I was right,' she said to Mum.

But on Tuesday Kitty had a bad day in school. She lost her pen, and somebody pushed her over in the playground, and she couldn't find her gym shoes, and – oh, lots of little things went wrong.

By the end of the afternoon her head was aching a bit, and she found herself thinking longingly of cuddling up with Mr Tubs in her little white bed. When the friendly clock on the mantelpiece showed her normal bed-time, Kitty nearly got up – then she remembered.

Dad and Mum were watching something boring on the television, and Daniel was doing his homework at the kitchen table.

Kitty stared at the screen, then at her book, but her head ached.

Still she wouldn't give in.

By the time it came to Thursday she felt tired. Very tired. 'Oh, Kitty, you've got dark circles under your eyes,' said her teacher.

'You keep yawning, Kitty,' said William – who looked as fresh as a daisy.

'Why don't *you* yawn?' she asked.

''Cos I'm not tired,' he said cheerfully.

'*Oh, I am!*' thought Kitty. But she didn't say it.

When Saturday morning came, Kitty slept and slept and slept.

She slept through her favourite cartoon programme on the television, which she was always allowed to watch.

She slept right through the cooked breakfast Mum always made on Saturday as a treat.

She slept, even though Dad called her loudly, and so he took Dan to the park for football without her.

By the time she came downstairs almost the whole of lovely Saturday morning had gone. The sun was shining in the garden, Dad and Daniel had gone – and Kitty felt she had missed out.

Mum was setting the table for lunch. She smiled at Kitty gently. 'It's not fair, you know,' she said.

'What's not fair?' Kitty asked.

'Well, what you've been doing is catching up on your sleep, because you simply haven't been giving yourself enough. And I don't think that's a *bit* fair, do you?'

'No,' said Kitty. 'It's not.'

It's not fair!

...that we can't stay

It was the summer holiday, and the most perfect one ever. Kitty's parents had rented a little cottage in the heart of the country. It wasn't big or grand: a sitting room, a kitchen, two little bedrooms and a bathroom under a thatched roof – that's all. But Kitty loved it.

She and Daniel had to share a room, which normally they hated – but that couldn't spoil their holiday. They hardly ever quarrelled – not *here*.

For two whole weeks she and Daniel ran wild, like little squirrels – climbing trees, playing hide-and-seek in the big garden, going for long walks in the woods with Mum and Dad.

'I've never had such a lovely time,' Kitty said.

But now it was the last day. Dad was sweeping the stone floor of the little kitchen,

and Mum was upstairs, packing their bags. It was over. And Kitty couldn't bear it.

Dad found her sitting by the sitting-room window, looking out across the fields, with a very sulky look on her face.

'Mum's calling you, Kit,' he said. 'You've to go and start packing your toys.'

Kitty said nothing.

'Come on – what's the matter?' asked Dad.

'Donwannagoback – noffair,' she mumbled, without turning round.

Dad laughed. 'What are you complaining about now?'

Kitty swung round to face him, and folded her arms. 'I said it's not fair we can't stay,' she said, crossly. 'I don't want to go back to our boring old house, in the boring old town, and go to boring old school. I want to stay here for ever and ever.'

'But you *can't*, Kit,' said Dad.

'I know – and it's not FAIR!' shouted Kitty, bursting into tears and running out of the room.

An hour later Dad carried the suitcases downstairs, and put them in the car. Daniel was helping. Mum was tidying the sitting room. But there was no sign of Kitty.

'Kitty!' Mum called, sounding worried.

'What's wrong?' asked Dad.

Mum rushed past him, and looked into the downstairs toilet. 'Oh, where *is* that girl?' she said.

They looked everywhere – under the beds, in the bathroom, in the wardrobe, behind the sofa, under the tables, even in the wicker basket on the landing. But there was no sign of Kitty.

Daniel called her name loudly.

'Oh . . . she wouldn't wander off and get

lost, would she?' Mum asked, in a very anxious voice.

'No way,' said Dad. 'She knows that would be wrong and silly, and I *know* she'd never do it. No – she's hiding, that's all. She doesn't want to go home.'

'Well, she's found a really good hiding place,' said Daniel, rather pleased at the thought that his sister was going to get into trouble.

'So how can we get her out of it?' murmured Dad. 'Hmm, maybe I've got a plan . . .'

At that moment Kitty was sitting in the one place they hadn't thought of looking: the little lean-to shed where old deck-chairs were kept. Or at least – Mum had just looked in quickly, peering through the dusty glass in the door. There was a spider's web over a hole in the glass. 'Ugh, Kitty would never go in there,' she thought.

But Kitty hid behind two stacked deck-chairs, feeling very pleased with herself. 'Now they won't be able to go,' she said to herself.

Just then she heard Dad calling. 'We're off now, Kit,' he shouted, 'so if you don't want to come with us, you can stay here.'

'Goodbye,' shouted Mum and Daniel.

'Ha, if they think I'd fall for that one . . .'

smiled Kitty. But then she heard the car doors slam, then the engine start, and then the sound of the car driving away. She waited for a while, not believing what she had heard.

It was quiet.

Very quiet.

Something rustled at the back of the shed, and a spider ran across the floor.

Kitty decided she had been in there long enough.

She crept from her hiding place, and stood listening. Not a sound. The holiday cottage that had been full of family noise was now silent and empty, and Kitty didn't like it. But she knew she had to be brave.

'Right then, I'll go and read my book in the sitting room . . . then I'll go for a walk, then . . .' she said, in a small voice.

It was so *very* quiet.

Slowly she walked up to the back door and pushed it open. It was funny – she had never noticed it creak like that before. In the kitchen the tap went *drip, drip, drip*. It sounded awfully loud in the empty house.

'Oh, dear,' said Kitty. 'I don't think I like it here any more.'

But what was that? Was it a sound. . .?

Slowly she pushed open the door into the little sitting room, and there she saw . . . Mum, Dad and Daniel, sitting on the sofa, grinning at her.

'OH!' cried Kitty, and ran into Mum's arms.

'We knew you'd come out,' said Daniel.

'As if we'd go and leave you,' said Mum.

'We parked the car outside the gate, and crept back,' said Dad.

Kitty was so relieved she didn't say

another word about staying, and Mum and Dad didn't tell her off for hiding.

But two weeks later it was her birthday. And Mum and Dad's present was very big.

Kitty was thrilled to see her very own little playhouse, with a painted thatched roof, and painted roses round the door.

'There you are, Kit,' said Dad. 'Now you've got your very own cottage, to have holidays in all year round!'

It's not fair!

...you always win!

It was such fun having a new friend next door. Kitty and William got on really well – most of the time. Every Saturday morning one of them would squeeze through the hole in the fence, and soon they would have a good game going.

That is – until they quarrelled. And as they knew each other better they started to quarrel more and more. It wasn't that they liked each other less. It was just that they were too alike. And both of them wanted to win. All the time.

Kitty would often come back from William's house sulking.

'Had one of your tiffs, dear?' Mum would say.

'They're just like an old married couple,' teased Dad – which made Kitty crosser than ever.

But soon she or William would feel bored.

So one of them would squeeze through the hole in the fence – and soon they would be playing again.

On this particular Saturday it was pouring with rain. Kitty pulled on her anorak, picked up a carrier-bag, stuffed it full of games, told her mum where she was going, and ran next door.

'What shall we play?' asked William.

'Snakes and ladders,' said Kitty.

But the red counter Kitty chose always seemed to land on snakes' heads, whilst

William's blue counter climbed up ladder after ladder.

At last – 'I've won!' – he cried.

Kitty said nothing – even when he won the second game as well.

Then they tried Ludo. This time Kitty chose blue for luck, and William swapped to green. But however hard she shook the dice, Kitty kept throwing ones and twos, whilst William threw sixes. The green counters raced around the board, and landed home, whilst the blue counters just couldn't get going.

At last – 'I've won!' – he cried.

Kitty said nothing, but her mouth turned down.

'What about snap?' asked William with a grin.

'Oh, all right,' sighed Kitty.

It was hopeless. William spotted the pairs so quickly, and yelled, 'SNAP!' so loudly – and soon he was sweeping up the pile. Kitty threw down her last card. Her face went red.

'It's not fair!' she shouted. 'You *always* win!'

'That's because I'm clever,' said William with a grin, flicking the pack of cards.

Kitty was so disappointed she wanted to cry.

Just then William's big sister Sally walked

past. She was thirteen, and *very* grown-up, and Kitty thought she was wonderful. Sally liked Kitty too – and she heard what William said.

'That's rubbish, Will,' she said. 'It's got nothing to do with being clever. You're just lucky.'

'No, it's *skill*,' boasted William.

'Doesn't take any skill to throw a dice,' snorted Sally.

'Whatever it is, it's *not fair*,' wailed Kitty.

'Crybaby,' said William.

At that, Sally took hold of Kitty's hand, and led her upstairs without another word. Her room was marvellous; full of beads and books and ornaments, with posters of pop singers and Sally's own bright paintings on the walls.

'Now,' said Sally, taking out a little chess set. 'William's just learning this. Can you play?'

'Dad started to show me, but . . .'

'Right. Now, you remember how each piece moves. . .?'

Kitty remembered, and soon she was absorbed in the game. Sally told her how to work out moves well in advance, and how to guess what the other person would do, and

when to move the King and the Queen. It was such fun – like fitting together the pieces in a jigsaw puzzle. Kitty loved it.

After nearly an hour had passed, Sally said, 'Now you go downstairs and challenge William.'

Kitty did just that.

They played in silence, concentrating really hard. At last William looked up with a frown. 'You're *winning*,' he said – as if he didn't believe it.

'Checkmate!' said Kitty.

'Not fair . . .' William started to moan.

'Too right!' said Kitty. 'It's jolly unfair that *some* of us have all the skill!'

It's not fair!

... that things aren't fair

It was a cold morning in November, and Kitty and her mum were walking along a busy road. They were going to see Gran, who lived in a special home for old people. Kitty liked visiting Gran. She always had a roll of sweets in her pocket.

Suddenly Kitty heard the sound of music. On the corner of the street stood an old man, playing a mouth organ. His clothes were worn. In front of him, on the pavement, was a battered hat, in which some people had put money.

He didn't play the mouth organ very well, and that made Kitty feel even more sorry for him.

'Mum, can we put some money in his hat?' she whispered.

'Of course,' said Mum, and pulled a silver coin from her pocket. Kitty felt embarrassed as she threw it down, and ran off quickly.

'Why is he poor, Mum?' Kitty asked.

'I don't know, love.'

Kitty said nothing.

As they waited to cross the road she noticed a huge poster on the wall opposite. It showed some children who were very, very thin, and was asking people to send money to help those children.

'Do they live in Africa, Mum?' Kitty asked.

Mum nodded. 'Well, *why* haven't they got enough food?' asked Kitty. '*We* have, so why haven't they?'

Mum sighed. 'Oh, I don't really know, Kitty. Sometimes it's because of the weather . . . it's all so complicated.'

Kitty said nothing.

Gran was in a good mood. She sat knitting, and her eyes sparkled when she saw them. 'How's my untidy little girl?' she said, reaching out to ruffle Kitty's hair.

'What are you knitting, Nana?' Kitty asked.

Gran held up a long shapeless-looking jumper. 'It's for your dad,' she said. 'It's his Christmas present.' Kitty imagined Dad wearing it, and giggled.

Soon she was quietly munching sweets, as Mum and Gran talked. But then she noticed that Gran didn't look so cheerful any more.

She was saying that she hadn't been well, and added, 'Don't worry, it's just old age, that's all.'

'You're not old, Gran – not *really* old,' Kitty said.

'Oh yes, I am,' sighed Gran.

Kitty wanted to go home, but felt guilty for thinking it. Later, when they did leave, she didn't want to look at all the other old ladies, waiting for their visitors. It made her feel sad.

All the way home she said nothing.

When they were sitting at the kitchen table Mum said, 'Come on now, Kit, what's the matter?'

'Why do people have to grow old? I don't want *you* to get old,' Kitty said.

'But I have to,' smiled Mum. 'We all have to.'

'Why can't we just all stay as we are?'

'Because we can't. It's not possible.'

Suddenly Kitty felt angry. She banged the table with her fist, so that all the cups and plates rattled.

'IT'S NOT FAIR!' she shouted.

'What isn't?' asked Mum.

'EVERYTHING. I feel so sorry for people like that poor man in the street, and then I think that we've got so much more than all those people in Africa and India, and I don't know why we haven't all got the same. And then Gran isn't very well, and I know she hates being old and not being able to do things . . . It's just not . . .'

Kitty felt like crying.

'Come on my knee,' said Mum. They had a big cuddle, then she whispered, 'Things do seem very unfair, don't they, love?'

Kitty nodded. 'But *why*, Mum?'

'I can't tell you. There isn't a grown-up in the world who could tell you the answer,' said Mum.

'I thought grown-ups knew everything,' sighed Kitty.

Mum shook her head. 'No, love. Oh, I *could* tell you that if we weren't so selfish we could give more to poor people – whether they live here or the other side of the world.

But there's more to it than that. And in any case, that wouldn't stop people being ill or old, would it?'

Kitty shook her head.

'I wish that *everything* was fair,' she said.

'So do I,' said Mum. 'But it can't be.'

'It still makes me cross,' said Kitty.

'And it probably always will,' said Mum.

It's not fair!

. . . she's got more presents

Christmas was the best day of the whole year, of course, and this time it seemed better than ever. Kitty's stocking had been crammed with funny little toys and jokes.

And after breakfast, when they opened their main presents, Kitty was so pleased. Mum and Dad had bought her what she most wanted: a huge art set, with lots of different paints, paper of all sizes, felt-tips, crayons, pencils and rubbers – all packed into a lovely carrying case.

She had plenty of books too, because she loved reading, and a lovely long scarf from Gran, in rainbow colours. Dan gave her three more soldiers and horses for her castle. She was very happy.

Kitty and Daniel were sorry about one thing, though.

This year Mum and Dad had arranged to go to have Christmas dinner with Aunty

Susan and Uncle Joe. *That* wasn't so bad, although they said they would rather have their own turkey.

But going to that house meant something that made them both moan.

'*Melissa*,' said Daniel, making a rude face.

'Yuk,' said Kitty.

They had to leave all the lovely clutter of wrapping paper and ribbons and glittery pom-poms, and go out. 'Aunty Susan's house is so *tidy*,' groaned Kitty in the car.

'Just like Melissa. Maybe she vacuum-cleans Melissa when she does the carpets,' grinned Dan.

Kitty giggled.

'That's enough,' said Dad.

There was a delicious smell of food when Aunty Susan opened the door. They all said Happy Christmas and hugged each other, although Daniel and Kitty ducked out of hugging their cousin.

'Why don't all the children play upstairs till dinner's ready?' said Uncle Joe.

But Dan asked if he could practise on his new skateboard on the garden path, and so Kitty was left with Melissa.

'Don't you like to wear your best dress on Christmas Day,' asked Melissa, 'instead of old jeans?'

'They aren't *old*, they're my new cords,' said Kitty indignantly. 'And this is a new jumper.'

'It wasn't a good start.

'Oh, well, I suppose you'd like to see all my presents,' said Melissa, throwing open her bedroom door.

Kitty gasped.

There was a toy cooker with plastic pots and pans, and a multi-way pram for Melissa's dolls, and a little pink wardrobe crammed with dolls' clothes on hangers, and a hairstyling set with pink plastic rollers, brushes and combs, and a funny dummy-head to work on.

'Who gave you all those?' asked Kitty.

'Mummy and Daddy. And I've got lots of

ordinary things like paints and books from
aunties and uncles.'

'Gosh,' said Kitty.

'What did you get?' asked Melissa.

Kitty told her.

'Is that *all*?' asked her cousin.

Suddenly Kitty felt like a balloon that has

gone pop. The turkey tasted delicious, and the crackers were fun, and Aunty Susan and Uncle Joe gave her a big notice-board in the shape of an elephant for her bedroom.

'So you can pin up your lists,' said Aunty Susan, picking up the paper right away and folding it neatly.

'Then you won't forget things,' smiled Uncle Joe.

Everybody laughed. Except Kitty.

At last it was time to go home. Kitty was glad to get back to their own comfortable, messy house. But Mum and Dad could tell that something was bothering her.

She sat by the Christmas tree, looking up at the coloured lights. And one thought was going through her mind – something so bad she wouldn't have told it to anyone. '*It's not fair she's got more presents than me.*' That was what Kitty thought.

Just then Dan came up. 'What did you think of Melissa's stuff then?' he asked.

'She had lots of nice presents,' said Kitty, in a small voice.

Daniel threw back his head and laughed. 'What? All those nimsy-mimsy things in pink plastic for dolly-wollies? Not your sort of thing, Kit. You've got more taste.'

And Kitty realised he was right. There wasn't a *single* thing in Melissa's room that she would have wanted. Not one.

She stared up at the tree again. It had a warm, Christmassy smell. Already, showers of little pine needles fell down when you touched it.

Aunty Susan had an artificial tree because she said real ones made too much mess. And they didn't have paper chains in each room, or a Christmas Candle in the window, dropping wax all over the place, but giving a warm welcoming glow.

Kitty grinned slowly.

'Our tree is *much* better than Melissa's tree,' she said.

And *Melissa* might have said, 'Not fair!'

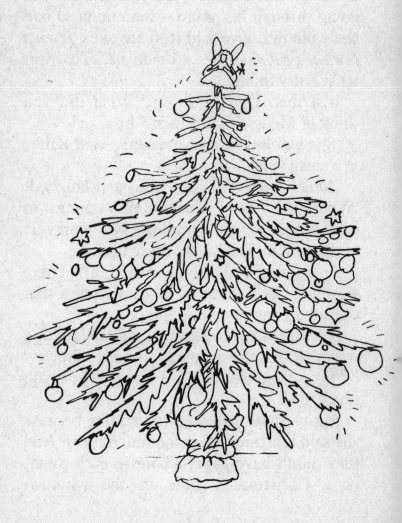

It's not fair!

. . . I have to do all the work

'It's your turn.'

'No, it isn't. I did it yesterday.'

'But you said you'd make up for that time last week when you went out.'

'Nonsense.'

It wasn't Kitty and Daniel who were squabbling. It was Mum and Dad. And Kitty and Daniel couldn't bear it.

They were arguing over who did the washing-up. Usually they took turns, but lately things had got mixed up – and now they were very cross with each other.

'Tired! Huh! It's just not fair that I have to do all the work,' said Mum.

'What do you think I do all day?' said Dad.

And so they went on.

And on.

Kitty and Daniel were listening in the hall. 'I wish they'd shut up,' said Dan.

57

'So do I,' said Kitty. 'Why do parents have to argue?'

Daniel shrugged. 'Dunno . . . I suppose it's because they're just the same as us, underneath.'

Then Mum swept past them, slamming the kitchen door behind her. 'I'm going out to my class, kids,' she said. 'Bye.'

A few minutes later Dad stomped from the kitchen. 'You can start getting yourself to bed now, Kitty, and it's time you did your homework, Dan,' he said grumpily. 'I'm going out into the garage to mend the car radio.'

juice, butter, eggs, and everything else on the table amongst the best china. And only one egg got broken. Just one.

She wiped down the shelves, and then left the fridge and freezer doors open wide. She had seen Mum do that. That was another job they wouldn't have to do.

After that Kitty went into the sitting room and plumped up all the cushions, pummelling them furiously so that clouds of dust rose into the air.

She ran the carpet-sweeper over the hall carpet, but forgot to put it away.

She grabbed the feather duster and attacked all the pictures, knocking most of them sideways as she did so.

And when Mum came through the front door, not long afterwards, Kitty was sitting on the floor surrounded by a pile of shoes, waving a brush, with polish all over her face and hands – and a lot of it on the floor too.

Dad must have heard Mum, because just then he came in through the back door. 'I just wanted to say I'm sor . . .' he began, then stopped. He looked around the kitchen in horror.

'What on earth has been going on?' he said.

Kitty beamed. 'Well,' she said, 'I hate it when you argue. And since you both think it's not fair that you have to do so much work, I thought I'd help you. *I've* done all the work!'

Dad went across and put his arms around Mum, who looked as though she might faint. They stared at each other for a long time. And then they began to laugh. And laugh.

'Are you pleased?' asked Kitty.

'Y-y-yes, darling,' spluttered Mum.

'And so you promise you'll never argue again?' said Kitty wagging her finger at them.

'If you'll never do the work again. Fair enough!' said Dad.